AF101177

# This Notebook Belongs To

____________________________________

www.ingramcontent.com/pod-product-compliance
Lightning Source LLC
La Vergne TN
LVHW060210080526
838202LV00052B/4237